Ernest J. Green

BIRTH ORDER, PARENTAL INTEREST AND ACADEMIC ACHIEVEMENT

San Francisco, California
1978

Published By

R & E RESEARCH ASSOCIATES, INC.
4843 Mission Street
San Francisco, California 94112

Publishers
Robert D. Reed and Adam S. Eterovich

Library of Congress Card Catalog Number
78-62231

ISBN
0-88247-544-4

Copyright 1978
By
Ernest J. Green

PREFACE

There exists in sociology a long history of concern with the family as a determinant of personality patterns, but only recently have sociologists been interested in position in the family as a possible influencing variable. The empirical study of birth order has recently taken on the quality of an almost frenetic search for possible correlates in attitude and behavior with different family positions, and lost time has been made up quickly. However, the birth order research has a disconnected character, almost all of it is atheoretical, and many conflicting findings appear in the literature. Birth order is a very accessible datum, and one suspects from many published reports a tendency to collect birth order information incidentally in connection with other research interests, and to make and publish comparisons with little emphasis on meaning and interpretation. Sorting through such literature in an attempt to unravel the meaning of family position as an influence on personality development can be a tedious and frustrating experience.

There are three steps involved in developing the area of birth order as an aid to understanding the socialization process: (1) it must be shown that the various ordinal positions experience different social learning experiences; (2) the different ordinal positions must be distinguished on meaningful aspects of attitude and behavior; and (3) a causal link between the early learning experiences and the later attitudinal and behavioral differences must be demonstrated. Most of the literature to date has concentrated on establishing correlations between birth rank and various types of personality measures and behavioral tendencies. We have some knowledge, although not extensive, of the different social environments provided for only children vs. first-born vs. later-born children. Other factors, such as spacing, and specific position (e.g. 2nd, 3rd, 4th etc.)

are probably important but little systematic data exist. Perhaps the most important shortcoming in the research at present, however, lies in the failure to provide a theoretical framework which would tie the diverse correlations together and link them to socialization experiences.

Order of birth is closely tied in with other features of family structure. Family size, sex of siblings and general social characteristics of the family also provide a social environment for the child and affect personality development. A more detailed statement of the major findings on these variables as they relate to the birth order research is available elsewhere (Green, 1970). The point here is that much of the empirical research has failed to control for these variables with the result that we often cannot ascertain whether a particular effect is due to birth order or some other family characteristic, or both. In addition, as Clausen notes (1966:9), the motivations and aspirations of parents for having large or small families and for spacing plans may be a contributing factor.

This paper reports a study of one relationship between birth order and an outcome variable. It seems probable that all the birth order relationships together, if fully explained, would account for only a small portion of the variance in human social behavior, and the limits on explanations which now exist, does the reason for birth order research become of much importance. If position in the family can tell us anything of significance about behavior, its study will have proved more fruitful than countless other ideas which have been discarded and forgotten.

I would like to acknowledge the assistance of Larry L. Hunt for the benefit of his ideas on this paper, and to Glenn L. Harper for his comments on what is now Chapter 2. Dr. Morris Rosenberg made the data available for analysis.

TABLE OF CONTENTS

Chapter		Page
PREFACE		iii
I.	THE RESEARCH PROBLEM	1
II.	A REVIEW OF BIRTH ORDER RESEARCH AND THEORY	4
	Birth Order and Family Size	5
	Birth Order and Sex of Siblings	7
	Birth Order and General Social Characteristics	10
	The Functions of Birth Order Research	11
	Substantive Findings and Interpretations	13
	Affiliation Need	15
	Other Hypotheses	17
	Summary	18
III.	THEORETICAL FRAMEWORK AND METHODOLOGY	20
	Symbolic Interactionism	20
	Hypotheses	25
	Description of the Data and the Sample	28
	Measurement of the Variables	30
	Data Analysis	32
VI.	RESULTS OF THE STUDY	35
V.	DISCUSSION AND CONCLUSIONS	54

		Page
APPENDIX A.	BIRTH ORDER RESEARCH BY SUBJECT AREA AND FINDINGS	63
APPENDIX B.	PARENTAL INTEREST INDEX	66
SELECTED BIBLIOGRAPHY		67

LIST OF TABLES

Table		Page
1.	Birth Order and Grades	36
2.	Grades and Birth Order by Sex	37
3.	Grades and Birth Order by Number of Children in Family (Males)	39
4.	Grades and Birth Order by Number of Children in Family (Females)	40
5.	Birth Order and Parental Interest	42
6.	Birth Order and Parental Interest (Males and Females)	43
7.	Birth Order and Parental Interest by Number of Children in Family	46
8.	Birth Order and Grades in Two Categories of Parental Interest	48
9.	Birth Order and Parental Emphasis	51
10.	Birth Order and Grades of Respondents Who Report Parental Emphasis on High Standards	52

CHAPTER I

THE RESEARCH PROBLEM

Birth order as a variable in the socialization process has received considerable attention in recent years. The assumptions underlying this literature can be summarily stated as follows: (1) the various birth orders experience different social environments; and (2) the differences in social learning experiences partially account for differences in behavior, personality characteristics or abilities.

From these assumptions, three goals have emerged: (1) to demonstrate that differences in social environments exist for different ordinal positions; (2) to demonstrate that individuals in the same ordinal positions are statistically different, in some way, from those in other ordinal positions; and (3) to establish a causal link between the social environment specific to an ordinal position and the personality attributes or behavior.

In a recent critique of birth order research, Kammeyer (1967) has charged that some explanations concerning why first-borns differ from later-borns are based on untested assumptions. The finding that first-borns exhibit superior academic performance, for example, is explained as a result of parents attaching greater significance to the birth and being of the first-born, and also that parents have more time and energy to devote to socializing the first-born child.

The finding that first-borns are academically superior, as a group, has been fairly well established (Elder, 1962a; Jones, 1956; Nisbet, 1961; Rosen, 1961; Sampson, 1962, 1967; West, 1960). Thus, the validity of a parental interest explanation depends in part upon whether the assumptions about the nature of parent-child interaction can be supported empirically. Put simply, the question becomes: Is it true that parents are more interested in and involved with first-born children?

Schacter (1959) has stressed this interpretation in his work. The tendencies exhibited by first-borns result from the fact that they enjoy a complete monopoly of their mother's attention at first. Even after the arrival of the second-born child, the first-born continues to have a certain priority, for he is treated with greater concern, affection and attention. For empirical evidence, Schater cites Sears, Maccoby and Levin (1957) who found that parents more eagerly anticipate the first pregnancy, that the first-born is weaned at a later age, and that the oldest is given more freedom in intra-sibling quarrelling.

The hypothesis that parental interest is greater for the first-born has not been directly tested, however. Empirical studies have been undertaken on questions of related interest, but the results are conflicting and difficult to interpret in terms of parental interest. Stout (1960) reports that each parent is more directive of the first-born than later-born child. Lasko (1954) failed to find support for the hypothesis that the parent interferes (consciously attempts to manipulate) less with the second child than the first. Sears *et. al.* (1957) found evidence that fathers, but not mothers, made more demands on the oldest than on the youngest child. The same authors report that the youngest of a larger family at five years of age is shown more warmth than the older siblings.

The conclusion must be that we do not know whether one birth order is favored by greater parental interest, and that the assumption is an hypothesis which deserves to be tested. An adequate answer to this question, furthermore, would state any qualifying conditions under which the assumption does or does not hold true.

In summary, the research problem can be stated as follows: (1) Given that first-borns are higher academic achievers, how can we account for the relationship? (2) Interpretations which account for the relationship by greater parental interest in first-borns rest on an untested assumption. Empirical evidence should be obtained to test this assumption. (3) Should the assumption be verified, we need to apply the parental interest factor directly to the relationship in question to find out whether parental interest can logically be used as an explanation.

CHAPTER II

A REVIEW OF BIRTH ORDER RESEARCH AND THEORY

A thorough review of the birth order literature lends credence to the charge made by Kammeyer (1967) that birth order research has been almost completely atheoretical. The empirical results available today have a disconnected character, in large part because they have not been theoretically motivated. Older studies noted in passing the remarks of Freud and Adler on ordinal position, while the more recent efforts have generally been interpreted as supporting, or modifying, or not supporting Schacter's arguments in The Psychology of Affiliation (1959). Many of the older reports were the results of serendipitous findings and, while today they are more likely to be planned, there is some question as to how much planning actually goes into birth order research. Judging from the number of reports stating that the birth order findings are part of a "larger" study concerned with another matter, what often apparently happens is that because birth order is an extremely accessible datum, questions on ordinal position are included perfunctorily on surveys and in experimental situations. After the relationship of primary interest has been analyzed, the dependent variable is run for birth order effects and a post hoc interpretation is made. This procedure has had two effects: (1) a large number of empirical findings have been reported; (2) the literature as a whole has a very disconnected character.[1]

Perhaps one of the major reasons so few theoretical statements about birth order are found lies in the intricate nature of the relations among birth order and other variables. Birth order is of interest because it is an empirical indicator. The underlying processes which ordinal position is assumed to indicate are influenced by other variables as well. Of all the influences upon socialization which could be working to interact with and modify positional effects we have empirical evidence (and much of it limited and inconclusive) on only three: family size, sex of siblings, and general social characteristics.

Birth Order and Family Size

Many researchers, especially recently, have shown an awareness that family size effects are closely interwoven with those of birth order. The socialization experiences of a child with four or five siblings as are the experiences of first from last-born children. In fact, there is some indication that comparisons of birth order without regard to family size may conceal more than they reveal. Bakan (1949) found that oldest children were significantly less likely, and youngest children significantly more likely, to be members of an alcoholic group, with family size uncontrolled. Navratil (1959) compared two child families and families larger than four children, and found the second born in the former and the last born in the latter were significantly more likely to become alcoholics. The most recent and most methodologically sophisticated study into this question (Smart, 1963) reported that birth order was *not* related to alcoholism when controlling for family size by comparing expected and obtained frequencies for each ordinal position. Persons from large families, however, are over-represented among alcoholics.

The relationship between ordinal position and social mobility is severely attenuated when family size is controlled. Svalastoga (1959) notes that because of the superior chances of children stemming from small families, single-born, first-born and last-born reveal slightly higher upward mobility rates than others. The author notes "when size of sibling group is held constant, no relationship between sibling rank and social mobility is discovered" (p. 404). Despite the author's conclusion, his tables do show a small, but consistent relationship with first-borns being slightly more mobile in every sibling category except one. This trend is also indicated in later studies (Elder, 1962; Yasuda, 1964; Alexander, 1968). The point of interest here, however, is not Svalastoga's conclusions, but the fact that his study is evidence for the necessity for considering family size when studying the effects of ordinal position on a dependent variable.

Exactly how family size and ordinal position are related to each other and to socialization and personality has not been specified for many situations. Two findings from the Roseberg and Sutton-Smith (1964) study of sex-role identification are of interest. One result was that "As family size increases, anxiety in first- and non-first borns tends to decrease" (p. 323). Thus, some factors may show a fairly straightforward and constant relationship when considering family size and ordinal position together. Other variables, however, show an interaction effect between family size and birth order. Another finding in the same study is stated as "the effects of ordinal position on sex-role identification vary with family size; i.e. varying dynamics are required to account for ordinal effects in two- and three-child families" (p. 325). Further findings in this study indicate that family size and ordinal effects may interact with sex of siblings to produce still different effects.

The major findings of family size which bear upon the effects of birth order are summarized below:

1. Family size is related to adjustment of children, with children of small families being rated better adjusted on the average (Damrin, 1949). Bossard and Boll (1956) report that in large family systems older children tend to overprotect younger children with unfortunate results.

2. The necessity for centralized leadership increases concurrently with the size of the family. The larger family is more likely to use sib-inflicted punishment for practical needs. (Elder, 1962b).

3. There is an increase in the mechanical method of introducing information and reaching a solution as size of family increases (Elder, 1962b), e.g., greater reliance on discipline by rules.

4. In the large family system (as compared with the small family), specialization of role is sib-assigned very early (Bossard & Boll, 1956).

In addition, two mechanical factors seem important in connection with family size. The larger the family, the more likely that any specified child will have an opposite-sexed sibling and the larger the family, the older (on the average) the last-born's parents will be.

Finally, Clausen (1966:9) has pointed out that family size can hardly be understood apart from the values and aspirations of parents. A major reason for family limitation is to be able to achieve a higher standard of living, and enjoyment or pronounced discomfort in the parental roles may influence decisions to have more children. So the effects of birth order are interwoven with the effects of family size and through family size, with more general social characteristics and motivational orientations.

Birth Order and Sex of Siblings

As is the case with family size, failure to consider the relationship between birth order and sex of siblings has led to problems of interpretation. Sex of siblings, for one thing, modifies the relationship between birth order and college attendance. Schacter (1963) and Bayer (1966) both reported an overrepresentation of first-born and only children in college populations. This finding, reported by others as well (see Appendix A for a summary) has been interpreted in terms of need achievement, economic factors, and greater expectations of parents for first-borns. Recently, Smelser (1968) compared the relationship between college attendance and birth order, holding sex of sibling constant. He found that first-borns attain significantly more education than their last-born siblings only when first-born and later-born are of the opposite sex. Further, reviewing three earlier studies, he discovered an overrepresentation of the cross-sex two-child family in three independent samples studying this relationship, which accounts for the consistency of the previous findings. Thus, it appears that the overrepresentation of first-borns in college is a function of no only ordinal position, but also of the sex of the subject and the sibling.

Also, failure to take sex of sibling into account may mask an important relationship between birth order and another variable. Rosenberg (1965) found little association between birth order alone and self-esteem. However, taking into consideration whether the subject had any brothers or sisters brought some interesting relationships to light. The most impressive finding was that younger minority males (boys with all older sisters) have the highest self-esteem across a variety of controls. Further, only children have higher self-esteem than others, and among only children it is the male who has the higher self-esteem.

The following findings with respect to sex of siblings seem to be important for birth order research:

1. For five and six year old children, both males and females with a male sib score higher than those with a female sib on a verbal intelligence test (Koch, 1954).

2. The female child with male siblings tends to assimilate role of opposite sex and hence shows more traits appropriate to the opposite sex (Brim, 1958, Rosenberg and Sutton-Smith, 1964). The picture

of the male child with female siblings is not clear because of conflicting results for the two studies.

3. For five and six year old children, those in cross-sex pairs are rated friendlier to adults than those in same-sex pairs (Koch, 1955).

4. In five and six year old children, second borns in the same sex-pairs are more insistent on their rights than first borns, in cross-sex pairs they were less insistent than first-borns (Koch, 1956a).

5. First-borns in cross-sex pairs had a greater number of interests and greater enthusiasm than those in same-sex pairs (Koch, 1956a; Sutton-Smith et. al. 1964).

6. The presence of an older like-sex sibling is conducive to appropriate sex-role identification with minimal anxiety; the presence of an older opposite-sex sibling leads to sex-role conflicts and heightened anxiety (Rosenberg & Sutton-Smith, 1964).

7. The presence of opposite-sex siblings tends to decrease the same sex preferences; the presence of like-sex siblings tends to reinforce the same-self preferences (Koch; 1954; Brim, 1958; Rosenberg and Sutton-Smith, 1964).

8. Each parent is most likely to be non-directive in child-rearing methods with a non-first child of his own sex (Stout, 1960).

9. Juvenile delinquency rates are higher for (1) males having younger sibs of each sex; (2) girls having all brothers, than any other constellation (Sletto, 1934).

There are also indications in the literature listed above that spacing, as well as sex of siblings, is a significant variable. However, research designs at present are not able to employ the number of controls required to take spacing into account.

One of the most ambitious efforts in explorations of the effects of birth order, family size and sex of siblings is a recent study by Sampson et. al. (1967). This study used a sample of high school children from two-sibling families, controlled for subject's sex and sex of siblings, and made several comparisons among the eight cells generated. One finding worth noting was that first-born males (but not females) manifest more achievement related conformity than second borns, a replication from an earlier study (Sampson, 1962) which did not employ the controls. The study furnishes added support for the interpretation that first-born females are more resistant to social influence than late-born females because of their differential involvement in rearing later-born sibs and an early introduction to the adult role, which give the female more training in independence.

Birth Order and General Social Characteristics

Findings on the relationship between birth order and general social characteristics are scattered and not very illuminating at present. That there are relationships seems apparent from the knowledge we do possess. For one thing, the size of a family is not independent of socio-economic characteristics, and Sears et. al. (1957) have shown that patterns of child rearing vary by socio-economic class. Elder (1962a), controlling on social class and family size, found that first-borns have higher academic motivation than youngest of family, with one exception being the lower class family with four or more children. This may or may not be a significant exception, but more widespread controls on social characteristics should allow a greater refinement of the emerging birth order principles. Kammeyer (1966) found that first-born college girls described themselves as more religious than did later-born girls. This, plus other findings in the study, led him to conclude that first-born children are "conservators of the traditional culture" (p.515). This hypothesis in effect predicts that birth order is related to a whole gamut of social characteristics known to correlate with conservatism, and should provide further incentive for implementing controls of general social characteristics.

Cross-cultural replications are relevant to the general question of social characteristics. Three studies were located which could be considered in terms of findings in the United States, Varela (1964), in a sample of Uraguayan high school students found support for the hypothesis that first-borns would tend to volunteer for group psychological experiments more often than later-borns, a finding reported in four U.S. college populations. Vuyk (1959) reports characteristics of older and younger brothers in two child families in Germany (anxiousness, introvertedness in first borns) which have been found in several U.S. studies. A sample of postgraduates from Calcutta University in India were administered questionnaires, and the results showed a preference for self-restraint as a motive for life in later-borns (Ray-Chowdbury, 1965). Although the language does not compare directly with that normally used in birth order research in the United States, this finding appears incompatible with attributes which have been assigned to later-borns from studies in this country.

The Functions of Birth Order Research

If the birth order research is to contribute substantive understanding to our knowledge of socialization and personality, three things should be demonstrated: (1) that the social environment and interaction processes are different for the various ordinal positions; (2) that individuals in differing ordinal positions behave differently and/or have different characteristics; and (3) that there is a connection, and exactly what the connection is, between the differing social environments and the personality characteristics and behavior.

The bulk of the birth order research to date has concentrated on demonstrating that significant statistical differences can be obtained for first-borns and later-borns. Appendix A lists the major areas of concentration and summarizes the findings for each area. Although differences have not been found in all areas and some areas show conflicting findings, the overall picture suggests that it is possible to predict many differences in first- and later-borns when dealing with statistical tendencies in large samples.

Secondly, there is evidence from the birth order literature that individuals do experience different social environments according to their ordinal position. Some of the better supported findings on this topic include:

1. In conversation, the family adjusts its linguistic level to the older children (Bossard, 1945).

2. First-borns and only children have more difficulty in learning age-subordination (Davis, 1941).

3. Parents behave more warmly toward second children than toward their first (Stout, 1960; Elder, 1962a; Lakso, 1954).

4. Parental control is more permissive toward second than toward first children (Stout, 1960; Elder, 1962b; Lasko, 1954; Sears, 1950).

5. The youngest child is more likely to perceive mother as principal disciplinarian (Henry, 1957).

6. The oldest is more likely to be breast or bottle-fed longer, and to undergo greater emotional upset at weaning (Sears et. al., 1957).

The third necessity, that of demonstrating which and how the interaction processes and social conditions differing for ordinal positions affect behavior and characteristics, has been met far less well. Two problems present difficulties in explanation. First, there is at present no theoretical perspective which accounts for all the findings. Second, longitudinal studies which could probably furnish the type of information needed, have not been undertaken with the express purpose of testing birth order propositions. Most of the interpretations in the literature which purport to explain the birth order findings must still be considered problematic and hypothetical.

In summary, the state of birth order research at this time closely follows a pattern similar to this example: The assumption is made that (a) parents attach greater significance and importance to the birth of their first-born child (an untested proposition). The researcher asks (b) what effect this will have on the child's behavior and psychological development and concludes that (c) parents should concentrate their expectations on the first-born and push for higher academic achievement. The operational hypothesis is stated as (d) a difference in the academic achievement of first-borns and later-borns. (e) The results of the study are in the predicted direction.

Regardless of how often this same reasoning is followed and the hypothesis supported, the important questions are left unanswered. Is (c) the result of (a)? If so, under what conditions does the relationship hold? Which variables intervene between (a) and (d), and what are their effects? These are the types of questions left unanswered by the birth order research at present.

Substantive Findings and Interpretations

The birth order findings have been summarized by subject area in Appendix A to this paper. Where the findings are consistent, the result has been furnished as a conclusion. This Appendix was developed as an aid, a device in evaluating the research, and should not be considered a definitive synthesis of the findings. In fact, considerable injustice has been done to the findings in this type presentation. The qualifications and interpretations of the authors represented have been ignored, and all findings have been reduced to their lowest common denominator, comparisons of first- vs. later-borns. Male-female differences are also ignored in the summary, except where a reversal of effects is supported, and in this case note has been made in the conclusions. The major purpose of Appendix A is to summarize a voluminous amount of research as concisely as possible so that an evaluation can be made and generalities noted.

In the twenty-one subject areas to which birth order has been related, six show conflicting and/or inconclusive results. In four other areas, only one study supports the conclusions; two further areas are supported by only two studies each. Thus, in over half of the twenty-one areas considerable caution seems warranted in terms of the inconclusive or poorly supported findings.

Any serious attempt at a synthesis of the findings, moreover, must consider the in congruity of results between areas. Can we explain why first-borns are more likely to attend college <u>and</u> less likely to become alcoholics? On the surface, there appears to be considerable incongruity between the findings in different areas. For example, the two conclusions--first-borns are more honest, and first-borns are overrepresented in delinquency rates--appear antithetical. One explanation may lie in the fact that first-borns are more responsive to normative influences (see Conformity). In the honesty study (Wuebben, 1967) subjects were asked not to reveal the purpose of a psychological experiment, and then later to indicate whether they had done so. Sletto (1934) analyzed records of delinquents and compared predicted with observed frequencies by birth order. If first-borns are most subject to normative influences, then we should expect to find first-borns overrepresented in delinquency rates <u>when</u> the sample is heavily weighted with children from a delinquent subculture, as Sletto's apparently was, because delinquency patterns are normative.

This principle of greater responsiveness to normative influences does not, unfortunately, make sense out of all the findings. The theoretical formulation which has generated the most interest in birth order research is the affiliation need hypothesis (Schacter, 1959). Schacter's formulation, once outlined, can be applied across the findings in different areas, as was done above, to determine its explanatory power.

Affiliation Need

In The Psychology of Affiliation (1959), Schacter presents the rudiments of a scheme for interpreting the meaning of birth order. His findings, and his interpretations, have been retested by many researchers since (many of the studies cited in Appendix A under achievement, affiliation, anxiety responses of children because of the mother's greater anxiety in relation to the first child (p. 43). Taking Sears (1950) hypothesis as a point of departure--that generous amounts of attention and love lavished on the infant, coupled with the frustration of infantile dependency needs, he reasoned that first-borns would experience conditions leading to the development of greater dependency needs. If dependency is a link, it should be expected that behavior derived from dependency should be related to ordinal position.

From a sample of college females, Schacter found (1) greater preference for affiliation on part of first-born is present only when substantial anxiety exists; (2) fear-arousing situations arouse more anxiety in first-born than in later-born; but (3) with equal anxiety, first-borns much more often choose togetherness. Also, his results showed that only children do not differ appreciably from first-borns (pp. 54-55).

Schacter cites several previous studies of birth order in his analysis. Briefly, they showed (1) no relationship between ordinal position and neurotic inventories; (2) first-born are more likely to go into therapy; (3) among fighter pilots in Korea, aces were more likely to be later-born; and (4) later-borns were more likely to become chronic alcoholics (p. 69).

In the chapters on Anxiety Reduction and Self Evaluation, Schacter drew two conclusions: (1) For first-born subjects, anxiety reduction is a consequence of being together with others in the same plight (p. 112); and (2) first-borns put more reliance on social means of evaluation than do later-borns (p. 131). The second conclusion drew heavily on Festinger's theory of social comparison.

Birth order has been used to explain variations in three areas: (1) overt behavior; (2) personality characteristics; and (3) ability. Affiliation most closely predicts behavior. From there, the inference has been made to personality (affiliation need). Affiliation as an explanation of specific abilities is most removed from the hypothesized connection between interaction processes and affiliation tendencies.

The birth order correlates of behavior are, on the whole, in the direction predicted by affiliation tendencies. Research specifically designed to test affiliative behavior has been positive when predicting that first-borns tend to affiliate to a greater extent than later-borns under stress.

Schacter's system is tied together by the dependency link. Behaviors derived from dependency, such as influencibility, should then be related to ordinal position. The conformity studies are generally consistent in showing that first-borns are more influencible <u>under certain conditions</u>. Reasoning one step further that greater influencibility means greater responsiveness to normative demands, Heiss (1960) found greater homogamy in religion for first-borns (homogamy can be considered a form of conformity). Wuebben (1967), as previously noted, found first-borns to be more honest.

The affiliation hypothesis appears to have far less utility in explaining abilities or skills appearing differentially in ordinal positions. One problem here is in squaring the conflicting propositions that oldest children are more dependent (Schacter, 1959) and yet are given greater independence training (Bossard & Boll, 1956). One indication that higher academic achievement does not follow directly from affiliation theory is furnished by Schacter's (1963) attempt to demonstrate that greater eminence in first-borns can be attributed to greater opportunity for higher education and less popularity with peers.

Other Hypotheses

Two other generalizing concepts have been employed in several studies to explain birth order correlates. The ideas deriving from need achievement and identification theory seem to offer alternatives to Schacter's explanation in some areas of birth order research.

Sampson (1962; 1967) has argued that early independence training is related to the development of need achievement (n Ach). There is a relationship between high n Ach and independence from influence; however, conformity for persons high in n Ach may be expected when conformity is perceived as leading to achievement. In addition to offering an alternative explanation to the conformity findings, this argument seems better equipped to explain the rather consistent overrepresentation of first-borns in academic achievement, and especially in academic motivation. This line of reasoning may be employed with respect to the findings on honesty, juvenile delinquency, religious homogamy, and personality traits (first-borns are more adult-oriented, later-borns are more peer-oriented).

Stotland and his associates (1962; 1963) have been using ideas derived from psychological identification models in interpreting birth order research. They found that later-borns have greater ability to empathize under a variety of conditions. Their work can be considered an extension of Schacter's original hypothesis, but it involves an extra dimension. Schacter posits a greater reliance on social means of evaluation for first-borns. The work on identification suggests that later-borns put more reliance on information for evaluation. The findings on role and sex-role identification make sense only when this extra dimension is considered.

Summary

Application of various theoretical perspectives to the birth order findings suggest that no one generalization at present is sufficient for explanation of all reported findings. This is due, no doubt, in part because of the differing definitions of operational variables, differing classification systems, and because of the conflicting findings in some areas. However, even concentrating only on those areas where findings are consistent and methods reasonably comparable, it seems unlikely that affiliation need, need of achievement or empathy processes contain a full explanation of birth order differences.

A secondary purpose of this paper is to suggest that the symbolic interactionist perspective, as a theoretical framework, can provide insight into the question of birth order. This framework has not been applied to birth order research previously. The following section will outline those aspects of symbolic interactionism which are deemed applicable to the study being reported and attempt to justify use of this theoretical orientation in birth order research.

FOOTNOTES -- CHAPTER II

1. In addition to Kammeyer (1967:71-73), this conclusion has been reached by Stroup and Hunter (1965:58).

CHAPTER III

THEORETICAL FRAMEWORK AND METHODOLOGY

Symbolic Interactionism

Symbolic interactionist theory developed in the United States from the cumulative writings of Cooley, Dewey, Baldwin, Thomas, Mead and others in the early part of the twentieth century. The most comprehensive formulation to date is contained in the posthumously published <u>Mind, Self and Society</u> (Mead, 1934).[1] The following presentation is an attempt to summarize briefly the major tenets of symbolic interactionism. Considering the diverse origins of the theory, it should come as no surprise that complete agreement on what constitutes the major concepts, premises and propositions of the interactionist position has not been reached.

Symbolic interactionism has been considered a middle-range theory (Dager, 1964: 744). Rather than attempting to encompass the full range of human behavior, the approach focuses upon human behavior that is distinctly human, or that which is not shared by man and the lower animals. The interactionist's range has boundaries outside which lie behavior that is studied by the biologist or the behavioral psychologist, and inside which lie a framework that is essentially social psychological.

The overall areas which have received the major share of attention in both theory and empirical research based upon the interactionist tradition are socialization and personality. The former process refers to how the individual acquires the attitudes, orientations and behavior characteristic of his society, and the latter process refers to the persistence and stability of these same components. Within these areas, the theory has traditionally limited consideration to the person within the "normal" range of development insofar as the development of propositions is concerned, with the assumption that the same underlying premises can serve as devices for exploration of tendencies considered outside the normal range by the individual's society.[2]

The basic assumptions of symbolic interactionism have been set down in detail by Rose (1962:5-18) and, in a more concise manner by Stryker (1964:134-136). Drawing two major, far reaching, assumptions from these sources, we can provide a general understanding of what guides the interactionist.

Assumption #1: "Society . . . . precedes any existing individual." (Rose, p. 13). The individual is born into a social group with shared values, ideals, norms -- culture. This implies that the most efficient way to approach the understanding of social behavior is through study of the society into which the individual is born. Two important implications underlie this assumption. First, since humans are the only culture-bearing species, a further assertion can be made that insofar as human behavior is a product of social interaction, there are principles of human social behavior that cannot be inferred from non-human forms. Secondly, the infant is born with the capacity to become human but becomes so only in interaction with socialized others.

Assumption #2: ". . . . the human being is actor as well as reactor." (Stryker, p. 135). Men do not respond directly to physical stimuli, for the physical world has been classified and categorized by use of symbols. If men respond to a symbolic environment and at the same time possess the capacity to create symbols, they can act in response to their own productions. The significance of this part of the assumption can best be appreciated by comparing it with the rigid behaviorism which reduces human behavior to a stimulus-response model, in which only reation is possible. Admittedly, a person is a reactor in the sense that he is born into a world which has been structured by others, but he becomes an actor by creating his own structure, selecting a hierarchy of others significant to him, and defining the social situations in which he finds himself.

The major concepts used by interactionists are an equally important aspect of the theoretical framework. In a review of developments in the theory since the late 1930's, Kuhn (1964) gives prominent places to the concepts of role, self and reference group. These concepts have played negligible parts in the study of ordinal position in the family, yet they seem well designed to furnish insight into the relationship between birth order and various dependent variables.

The concept of role has been sharpened by the analysis of Turner (1962), who distinguished between the Lintonian role conception as conformity and the Meadian view of role as process. The former model views roles rigidly as "a set of prescriptions inherent in a position" (Turner, 1962: 25). The structure of an individual's behavior is preformed by societal role-scripts which allow for little improvization. The Meadian model, in contrast, provides the basis for a viewpoint of role which ". . . . shifts emphasis away from the simple process of enacting a prescribed role to devising a performance on the basis of an imputed other role" (Turner, 1962: 23). The individual engages in an active type of behavior, continually testing inferences about the nature of the complementary roles in the interaction process. Rather than constituting rigid scripts for behavior, roles constitute a perspective from which to view the ongoing interaction situation.

First-borns tend to behave in ways that are similar partially because they have been exposed to similar role learning experiences. Viewing role in the Linton sense causes some problems in application to a position such as first-born. Inasmuch as social interaction takes place constantly throughout life, the personality undergoes continual modification. The amount of modification in a highly stable, remote, isolated culture of the type studied in much anthropological field work is likely to be minimal. The modification is likely to take place at a rapid rate when roles become more complex and unrelated, as in modern industrial society. If we utilize the Lintonian concept of role to explain similarities in the behaviors of those who share ordinal position, the problem arises of specifying exactly what the prescriptions for the position are. In fact, we are only beginning to uncover the tendencies that characterize ordinal positions. The Meadian conception of role, on the other hand, permits us to take advantage of the role concept by relating aspects of the social interaction situation, which are similar for ordinal positions, to personality.

As an example of such application, Brim (1958) used role-learning theory to predict that cross-sex siblings would assimilate opposite sex traits to a greater extent than same-sex siblings. Although parents are assumed to be major sources of sex-role learning, almost every child has a mother and father to learn from. Variations in type and amount of sex-role learning must occur on top of this base. These ideas received support in Brim's study of the two child family.

First-borns are also likely to behave in similar ways because they have similar concepts of self. They are more likely to move to the fore in certain types of social situations not only because they are accustomed to caring for younger siblings, but also because they have come to think of themselves as persons who take the initiative. Self theory has been one of the most popular approaches to understanding behavior in symbolic interactionism, but again, the concept has not been widely utilized in birth order research.

The self is assumed to be a product of social interaction. Cooley's theory of the looking-glass self (Cooley, 1922: 152) and Mead's principle of the reflexive self (Mead, 1934: Part II) suggest that attitudes toward the self are formed through the imagined evaluations of others. The concept one has of self is significant because the human actor can view himself as an object. As an object, the self lies at the center of the social system which constitutes the individual's environment, and as a central object, has greater salience and value for the individual. Further, it is assumed that an individual's organization of attitudes, or self, is correlated with how the person will behave in a social situation.

Propositions surrounding the origin of the self and self as a process in social interaction have been supported by research. Miyamoto and Dornbusch (1956), in a study of members of fraternities and sororities, found that when individuals were asked to rate themselves and others on self-esteem factors, their self-ratings were more influenced by what they thought others felt about them than what others actually did feel.

A third major concept in the interactionists' framework is the idea of a reference group hierarchy.[3] The reference group concept takes note of the fact that it is not merely membership in a group which determines behavior, but the nature of psychological identification with the group. Social processes such as status striving or the "passing" of a minority group member can hardly be attributed to behavior emanating from the standards of the individual's membership group.

Until adulthood, members of the family of orientation hold a prominent place in one's hierarchy of significant others. It follows, then, that the quality of parent and child interaction is an important variable for understanding behavior and the stability and organization of attitudes. This aspect of symbolic interactionism, as with the other major concepts, appears highly consistent with the lines of reasoning underlying the birth order research. Ordinal position has generally been assumed to be an indicator of underlying social processes, and a focus on processes has been on of the trademarks of interactionism.

Hypotheses

The findings that first-borns as a group exhibit higher academic performance than later-borns constitute a relationship that deserves explanation. But birth order itself possesses no explanatory power -- at most it is merely a rough empirical indicator. Interpretations in the literature suggest that a greater parental interest may account for the relationship (Bossard and Boll, 1956; Rosen, 1961; Sears et. al., 1957; Koch, 1954; Schoonover, 1959; and Lasko, 1954). Although the assumption of a relationship between birth order and parental interest has not been adequately tested, the literature is suggestive.

Several factors point to the proposition that first-borns, especially males, should report a higher degree of parental interest than later-borns. Bossard (1954) found that families tended to adjust the linguistic level in the family to the older child. Younger children may perceive this as greater parental interest in the older child. The Sears et. al. (1957) finding that parents more eagerly anticipate the first pregnancy is also suggestive in the same direction. Also, it has been suggested that vestiges of primogeniture remain in family attitudes in the United States today (Yasuda, 1964). To the extent that families do concentrate their resources toward educating the first-born male, this should also contribute toward an interest differential in favor of first-borns.

The position of only children with respect to expectations for interest of parents seems clear. Only children face no competing demands on parents' time from siblings.

All the parents' chips are on the one child, and as a result, this group should perceive and report the highest rates of parental interest. Other studies have grouped only and first-borns together to make comparisons (Schacter; 1959: 61, argues that only and first-borns do not differ significantly on important psychological tendencies). Here, it seems to make more sense to consider only children as a special case, and to expect that parental interest should be more pronounced for this category.[4]

At this point, it seems pertinent to discuss further the nature of parental interest. What exactly is there in parental interest that relates to academic achievement? One possibility is that if parents are more likely to interact verbally with first-borns and only children, this could be an advantage in mental development and thus in academic performance. Yet the evidence suggests that no birth order differences exist for performance on verbal intelligence tests.[5]

There are other interaction processes implied by parental interest which may be directly related to academic performance, such as helping with homework and answering questions. However, many of these functions are performed for later-borns, but probably more often by older sibs. In fact, it has been argued that later-borns have a greater opportunity to learn skills related to academic performance from older siblings, and first-borns actually experience less anticipatory socialization and so should be in a relatively inferior position in the classroom (Berelson and Steiner, 1967: 179).

Investigators who have focused upon the symbolic, as opposed to the physical and mechanical aspects of interaction, suggest that the parent and child relationship could have a meaning with consequences greater than those suggested above. One finding suggests that parental interest is directly related to the evaluative component of the self concept (Rosenberg, 1965: 145). Furthermore, Katz (1967) reports that lower school achievement is associated with a propensity for self devaluation, and Rosenberg (1965: 119) found that the higher a student's grade average, the more likely the student would have a positive self evaluation.

Thus, the significance of parental interest for the child's academic performance may lie in large part in the fact that interest is interpreted as a positive evaluation, and parental disinterest as a negative evaluation. According to the Meadian conception of the development of the self, the negative evaluation from a significant other should be internalized as a negative self evaluation. Since positive self esteem has been found to relate to high academic performance and first-born and only children have been found to be academically superior, we conclude that a positive relationship between being first-born or an only child and experiencing less parental disinterest is predictable from the symbolic interactionist perspective.

If the argument which has been formulated is essentially accurate, several relationships among variables are suggested. This study will test three hypotheses bearing on these relationships, and attempt to specify the conditions under which the relationships do or do not hold. The hypotheses, and the reasoning upon which they are based, are as follows:

Hypothesis #1: Self reports of academic performance will be highest for only children, next highest for first-born children, and lowest for later-born children. This finding is expected in view of the consistency with which other investigators have reported a differential between first- and later-born respondents in academic performance. The prediction that only children will report higher grades than other positions follows from two factors. First, we have argued that it makes sense to consider only children an accentuation of the first-born positional effects where parental interest is concerned. Second, if parental interest implies positive self evaluation, which is in turn linked to higher academic performance, the Rosenberg (1965: 108) finding that only children have higher self-esteem than other positions lends credence to the prediction.

Hypothesis #2: Evidence of parental disinterest will be highest for later-born children, next highest for first-born children, and lowest for only children. (2a) This prediction should hold for both males and females, but differences for males should be more marked. This prediction is based upon the studies previously reviewed (see pp 25-26), most of which suggest this differential, and upon the expectations for parental interest which follow from the symbolic interactionist perspective.

Hypothesis #3: Holding parental interest constant, the relationship between birth order and academic performance will be eliminated or substantially reduced. If parental interest is a factor in the relationship between birth order and academic performance, then by comparing only those subjects for whom there is evidence of parental disinterest we will eliminate this factor and thus eliminate the relationship. Because the measure of parental interest groups respondents into only two categories, a complete elimination of the birth order effects is not expected. However, the control should produce at least an attenuation of the birth order effects if the prediction is to be supported.

With the hypotheses and their derivations listed, we turn now to the tasks of operationalizing the variables and explaining the measurements.

Description of the Data and the Sample

The study being reported here consists of a secondary analysis of data collected in 1960 under the direction of Dr. Morris Roseberg, NIMH. The interested reader is referred to Rosenberg's <u>Society and the Adolescent Self-Image</u> (1965) for a full description of the sample characteristics and data collection procedures (see especially Rosenberg's Appendix A). A brief description of the sample and data collection methodology follows as an aid toward interpreting the results of the present study.

The original sample was a random sample of eleven public day high schools in New York State, stratified by size of community. Stratification by other characteristics, such as socio-economic status, religion and nationality was not attempted. Of the eleven randomly selected high schools, ten actually participated in the study.

Data collection was accomplished through the high school principals and superintendents, with the actual administration of the questionnaires being conducted by the classroom teachers. The questionnaires were anonymous, and three separate forms were administered to all junior and senior students present on the day of administration. Each of the three questionnaire forms was alternately distributed. From the questionnaires returned, a total of 5,024 were retained after screening out forms which had not been answered seriously. Questionnaire responses were coded, keypunched and these operations were verified.

Despite the fact that schools were randomly selected, the sample cannot be considered representative of all New York State adolescents in the junior and senior age range. Omitted from the survey were students in parochial and private secondary schools, students who had dropped out of school before their junior year, and students who were absent on the day of administration of the questionnaires.

The sample of the present study consists of approximately one-third of the 5,024 questionnaires distributed by Rosenberg. These questionnaires contained information concerning the variables of interest -- birth order, family size, sex, parental interest and grades -- for the purpose of this study. This information was combined on one card deck for 1,450 respondents, and this deck represents the sample used herein. Since the questionnaire forms were administered to every third student alternately, there is no reason to suspect that the characteristics of this subsample of 1,450 differ systematically from those of the total sample. The same characteristics and omissions are therefore assumed to apply to this subsample and should be considered in interpreting and generalizing from the present analysis.[6]

Measurement of the Variables

The same source (Rosenberg, 1965) offers a more comprehensive explanation of the logic and methodology involved in measurement of variables being considered in this paper. (See Rosenberg's Appendix D for a listing of all scales and scoring included in the original study.) The following summary is intended as an aid in interpreting the present study.

This study concerns the relationships among three variables -- birth order, grades, and parental interest. The birth order variable was determined by a self report of the respondent. For comparisons, birth order has been classified into three categories -- only children, first-born and later-born. This categorization is deemed appropriate for several reasons. First, most previous studies on the same topic have used a similar system of categories, and having an analgous system should aid in making interpretations from the literature. One difference is that few previous studies have treated only children as a separate category. There is some reason to believe, however, that grouping only and first-borns into one category may mask important differences between these groups. Eisenmann and Taylor (1966) found that first-borns and only children possess significantly different MMPI profiles. Also, Rosenberg (1965: 108) reports that only children possess higher self-esteem than children with siblings. Other studies have suggested that birth order differences may exist in all positions, but a practical consideration prohibits comparison of each ordinal rank separately. The statistical comparisons which are appropriate to the data require a large number of cases in each category, and if controls are to be implemented many comparisons would become impossible if the categories were defined in a broader manner. The birth order categories to be used represent something of a compromise between the ideal and the minimum acceptable.

Measurement of grades is also based upon a self-report by respondents. Students were asked to indicate approximate letter grade average or numerical grade average. The later, where indicated, was converted to an appropriate letter grade. Some of the comparisons to be reported will present grades in three, rather than the standard five categories. The combination of grades into this threefold classification consists of A and B = High; C = Medium; and D and F = Low. This combining of responses was necessitated for some comparisons because of low numbers appearing in the F category.

A measure of parental interest was developed from three of the items appearing on one form of the questionnaire. The instructions governing responses to these items directed the respondent to think back to age 10 or 11, and to answer in terms of his experience at that time. The items are reproduced in Appendix B, along with an indication of how they are scored. Because the data indicated a very small number of respondents reporting extreme parental indifference, the scoring system is very liberal. That is, any response which could be interpreted as disinterest has resulted in the respondent's classification under "some evidence of disinterest." This category of respondents, by using the scoring system in Appendix B, was made large enough to allow for controls in making comparisons with respondents for whom there is no evidence of disinterest.

Data Analysis

Of the three variables of interest in this study, two are represented by nominal and one by ordinal level data. Birth order and parental interest will be treated as classification systems, and distributions of self-reported grades as measurement at the ordinal level.

The assumption that reported grades represent ordinal level data appears warranted for three reasons. First, the cross-classification of grades and other variables in this study is generally consistent with what other researchers have found or what we expect theoretically. Second, the question of whether the categories of A through F actually reflect an ordering of some underlying attribute such as ability or knowledge is of minimum importance in this study. Grades are used as if they have this property, and the question of interest is why some birth orders are more likely to appear in some of the categories than others. Furthermore, as explained earlier, some of the comparisons have collapsed the grades into three categories, thus reducing any error which may be present in the ordering.

Statistical analysis for testing the hypothesis is based largely upon the chi-square test for contingency tables. Chi-squares have been computed for all comparisons when the dependent variable is represented by nominal level data, and in some cases when the dependent variable is ordinal and a more refined analysis would add nothing to the comparison. Yates' correction for continuity has not been applied to the chi-square analysis. Guilford (1964: 237) contends that the correction is relatively unimportant when cell frequencies are 10 or greater. None of the comparisons yielded a chi-square which turned out to be near the division of a critical region.

When the dependent variable is represented by data at the ordinal level, a non-parametric test for ordered data usually has more power than chi-square (Blalock, 1960: 190-193). Blalock argues that the Kolmogorov-Smirnov test is the most appropriate of the non-parametrics for ordered data grouped into four or more large categories with a large number of ties (Blalock, 1960: 203). This test has been used for analysis when the independent variable is nominal and the dependent variable ordinal.

In some instances, when more than one control is employed, the cell frequencies have become too small for a chi-square analysis. In these cases, interpretations have been made from trends in the percentage distributions. The statistic which could have been used, Fisher's exact test, was considered unnecessary and perhaps misleading. Birth order effects are generally too small to appear statistically significant with a small number of cases. The chi-square results have been reported as insignificant whenever the probability of occurence through sampling error is greater than .10.

FOOTNOTES -- CHAPTER III

1. Although Mead's book contains the most important presentation of the theoretical formulations known as symbolic interactionism, many have noted the expository problems of this work, primarily that it is unintegrated and couched in non-operational language. Also, the past thirty-five years have seen both extensions and additions to the theory. The present account borrows liberally from several contemporary reviews and summaries of symbolic interactionist theory, including Rose (1962), Kuhn (1964a), and Stryker (1964).

2. Becker's classic treatment of the social learning experiences involved in marihuana use, for example, utilized the framework of symbolic interactionism (Becker, 1953). Deviance and conformity are merely two facets of the same problem for the interactionist.

3. For a detailed discussion of the development, use and problems involved in this concept, see Kuhn (1964b).

4. Warren contends that only children and first-born with siblings should be differentiated for all comparisons (Warren, 1966: 49).

5. Helen Koch's data showed that first-borns at six years of age scored higher than six year old later-borns on the Primary Mental Abilities Test (Koch, 1954: 220). The complete monopoly of the parents time that the first-born enjoys for a high proportion of the first six years may explain this. However, the Thurstone and Jenkins (1932) sample used older children and indicated that later-borns catch up and surpass first-borns on intelligence by age 18. Jones (1933) questioned the latter findings, claiming that when methodological difficulties are eliminated, no birth order differences in intelligence appear. Schoonover (1959) has reached the same conclusion. In any event, intelligence differences do not appear to be the explanation for the greater academic success of first-borns.

6. A further characteristic of the sample, of some interest because of the birth order variable, was pointed out by Dr. Rosenberg in a private conversation. The proportion of first-born to later-born is greater than would be obtained in a random sample of the total population today. The respondents surveyed in 1960 were products of the period known as the "baby boom" after the end of World War II. A similar group, in terms of age, would not show the baby boom effects if surveyed today or before 1960, and the samples would thus produce a proportionally greater number of later borns.

CHAPTER IV

RESULTS OF THE STUDY

Hypothesis # 1 predicts a relationship between birth order and grades with only first-born and later-born reporting differentially higher grades in that order. The comparison for the entire sample is summarized in Table 1. In general, the results follow the pattern expected, and one which is consistent with other studies. Only children are most likely to make high grades, with later-born children least likely to make high grades, and first-born in a middle position. Later-born children are overrepresented with respect to both medium and low grades.

A comparison of grades and birth order by sex indicates that it is primarily males for whom the relationship holds. Table 2 indicates that females report slightly higher grades than males in every birth order category, as the cumulative propostions tend to rise more rapidly for males than for females. This is true for every grade level in every birth order category except the grade of B for only children. The sex difference in later-born children appears to be the most marked difference. Only 31% of the later-born males report grades above C, as compared with 40% of the later-born females.

Within each sex, birth order differences with respect to grades still appear, but the differences are significant only for two comparisons within males. The differences in grades between first- and later-born females are consistently higher in each category for first-borns, but the differences are small. The differences between only and first-borns females are both small and inconsistent. Likewise, only and first-born males do not differ appreciably. The comparisons indicate, however, that later-born males are

Table I - Birth Order and Grades

Grades	Only	First-Born	Later-Born	
High	49%	45	39	
Medium	38	43	45	
Low	13	12	16	
Total				
Percent	100	100	100	
Number	185	567	701	1,453

Total $X^2 = 8.78$, 4 df, $p. < .10$

Table 2 – Grades and Birth Order by Sex

Grades	Only	Cum. Prop.	Males First-Born		Later-Born		Only		Females First-Born		Later-Born	
A	8	1.00	12	1.00	17	1.00	5	1.00	28	1.00	18	1.00
B	35	.92	111	.96	98	.95	42	.95	106	.90	139	.95
C	37	.55	127	.58	169	.69	35	.47	118	.51	149	.54
D	17	.18	38	.14	71	.22	6	.07	21	.08	35	.11
F	0	0.00	4	.01	11	.03	0	0.00	2	.007	4	.01
Totals	97		292		366		88		275		345	

Kolmogorov-Smirnov Results:

Comparison	D	X^2	df	Significance	D	X^2	df	Significance
Only/First-Born	.04	.46	2	NS	.05	.69	2	NS
First-Born/Later-Born	.11	7.86	2	p. 02	.05	1.55	2	NS
Only/Later-Born	.14	7.36	2	p. 05	.07	1.37	2	NS

more likely to make lower grades than either only or first-borns.

Other investigators have found that children from large families are less likely to make high grades in school (Elder, 1962a; Douglas, 1964). Since later-borns are more likely than first-borns to be members of families larger than two, this could conceivably account for the relationship between birth order and grades. Tables 3 and 4 compare birth order and grades within three family sizes.

Although the relationship is by no means linear, the general trend suggests that both first-born and later-born males have a decreasing chance of attaining high grades as family size increases. Within each family size, however, the birth order effects are still apparent. First-borns are more likely to report high grades, and less likely to report low grades than later-borns, regardless of family size. Birth order effects are not statistically significant within the three and four child family. Whether this is a meaningful exception in the relationship is difficult to ascertain, but one indication that it is not is furnished by the fact that the same exception is not present in Table 4, for females.

Size of family also has an effect on grades for females. Interpretation of Table 4 becomes somewhat problematic because of the small number of first-born females in families with five or more children. Grades tend to decrease somewhat as family size increases, but there are exceptions. Also, birth order effects within family size are less marked than for males. Within the two child family, the relationship between grades and birth order is in the opposite direction from other family sizes of females, and is in an opposite direction for the same family sizes for males. Later-born females in the two child family report more high grades and fewer low grades than do first-borns. Apparently, this reversal of birth order effects in the two child family is responsible for the failure of a relationship between birth order and grades to appear for the females as a whole in

Table 3 — Grades and Birth Order by Number of Children in Family (Males)

Grades	Family Size					
	Two		Three and Four		Five and Above	
	First-Born	Later-Born	First-Born	Later-Born	First-Born	Later-Born
High	43%	30	42	38	37	21
Medium	43	46	41	41	53	54
Low	14	24	17	21	10	25
Total						
Percent	100	100	100	100	100	100
Number	171	125	102	160	19	81
	$X^2 = 7.90$, 2 df, $p. < .02$		$X^2 = .76$, 2 df, NS		$X^2 = 15.89$, 2 df, $p. < .001$	

Total $X^2 = 24.55$, 10 df, $p. < .01$

Table 4 — Grades and Birth Order by Number of Children in Family (Females)

	Family Size					
	Two		Three and Four		Five and Above	
Grades	First-Born	Later-Born	First-Born	Later-Born	First-Born	Later-Born
High	50%	53	49	43	40	39
Medium	41	42	45	43	50	45
Low	9	5	6	14	10	16
Total Percent	100	100	100	100	100	100
Number	150	114	105	167	20	64
	$X^2 = 2.13$, 2 df, NS		$X^2 = 4.06$, 2 df, NS		$X^2 = .62$, 2 df, NS	
Total			$X^2 = 6.25$, 10 df, NS			

the sample.

Hypothesis #1 is only partially supported by this analysis and needs refinement. The relationship between birth order and grades is in the direction predicted, but is only of marginal significance for the entire sample. When sex of respondent is controlled, the birth order effects are significant only for males. The significance of the birth order effects remain for males when family size is controlled, while for females this control produces inconsistent trends for birth orders between families of varying sizes. Thus, the effects of birth order on grades appear to be only for males, and only between only or first-born and later-born males. The differences between only and first-born, while consistent for males, are small.

Hypothesis #2 predicts that respondents will report parental disinterest differentially, with only children reporting least, first-born children in an intermediate position, and later-born children reporting most parental disinterest. There is also some reason to believe that the differences should be greater for males than for females (hypothesis 2a).

Comparing all cases for which there is some indication of parental disinterest with all cases for which no evidence of disinterest exists, some modest differences appear in the birth order categories. Only children are the least likely, first-borns next, and later-borns most likely to report disinterest. As Table 5 indicates, these differences, though small, are statistically significant for the whole sample.

The expectations that the birth order -- parental interest relationship would be greater for males than for females was not met. Table 6 compares the male and female relationship separately and few differences are evident. The distribution of parental interest for first-born and later-born males and females is almost identical. Only females report a greater parental disinterest than only males, but even here the differences are

Table 5 - Birth Order and Parental Interest

	Only	First-Born	Later-Born
No Evidence of Disinterest	62%	59%	53%
Some Evidence of Disinterest	38	41	47
Total			
Percent	100	100	100
Number	172	474	577

$$X^2 = 6.25, 2 \text{ df}, p. < .05$$

Table 6 — Birth Order and Parental Interest (Males and Females)

	Males			Females		
	Only	First-Born	Later-Born	Only	First-Born	Later-Born
No Evidence of Disinterest	64	58	53	58	60	53
Some Evidence of Disinterest	36	42	47	42	40	47
Total						
Percent	100	100	100	100	100	100
Number	95	233	287	77	241	285

$X^2 = 3.31$, 2 df, NS $X^2 = 3.00$, 2 df, NS

not large and are based on fewer cases than the other birth order categories.

There are two possible interpretations for the failure to find significant sex differences in reported parental interest for different birth orders. Either primogeniture is not a factor for the present sample, or primogeniture manifests itself in a fashion which is not interpreted as a difference in parental interest. A more objective measure of parental interest, such as financial assistance from parents for college attendance, might well uncover differentials between first-born males and females.

The types of questions used to ascertain parental interest suggest the need to employ a control on family size. If we ask whether father and mother know most or only some of the child's friends, it seems reasonable to assume that knowledge of friends will decrease as the number of children increases. When a child of a large family reports that his parents know few or none of his friends, this may be interpreted by the child as lack of parental interest, but the influencing factor is family size rather than position in the family. With family size controlled, the difference in parental interest could still show up in a birth order comparison because later-borns are more likely to be members of a larger family.

To test this possibility, the birth order comparison was made with size of family controlled (Table 7). If family size is the determinant of parental interest, the birth order--parental interest relationship should disappear. In fact, this is what happens for families with more than two children.

With regard to how parental interest is perceived, only in the two child family does it seem to matter whether a child is first- or second born. This finding is of interest for two reasons. First, it suggests that parental interest alone may not be a sufficient explanation of the tendency for first-borns to report higher grades. The birth order effects on grades remained when controlling on family size for males, yet there are almost no birth order effects in larger family sizes on parental interest.

Secondly, the findings are similar to one of the results reported by Smelser (1968: 298). This study suggested that the overrepresentation of first-borns in college attendance is significant only in the two child family, and then only when first-born and later-born are of the opposite sex. The dynamics of family interaction may be qualitatively different in the two child and larger families. Any birth order comparison which concentrates solely on the two child family may in fact be accentuating differences, and any which compare birth order without regard to family size may end up masking any differences which are significant.

Hypothesis #2, that only and first-borns will report less parental disinterest than later-borns, finds some support in the comparisons but requires qualification. First, no sex differences were noted for the birth order -- parental interest relationship as anticipated. Secondly, in larger families, the ordinal position seems to be unimportant in perception of parental interest. Thus, the original hypothesis holds for both males and females, but is significant only in the two child family.

Having investigated the relationship between birth order and grades (Table 1, page 36), and the relationship between birth order and parental interest (Table 5, page 42), an examination of the meaning of these relationships can be undertaken. If the finding that only and first-borns report higher grades as a result of the lesser parental disinterest reported by these respondents, then controlling on parental interest should eliminate or substantially reduce the relationship between birth order and grades. Thus, hypotheses #3 predicts that when controlling on parental interest, a significant relationship between

Table 7 – Birth Order and Parental Interest by Number of Children in Family

	Two		Family Size Three and Four		Five and Above	
	First-Born	Later-Born	First-Born	Later-Born	First-Born	Later-Born
No Evidence of Disinterest	61%	51	55	55	56	53
Some Evidence of Disinterest	39	49	45	45	44	47
Total Percent	100	100	100	100	100	100
Number	264	199	178	269	32	114
	$X^2 = 3.09$, 1 df, p. $<.10$		$X^2 = 0.00$, 1 df, NS		$X^2 = .16$, 1 df, NS	

birth order and grades will not appear. Table 8 reports the results of the comparisons for this hypothesis.

Technically, no support can be claimed for hypothesis #3. Since what is being tested is the effect that controlling on parental interest has on the relationship between birth order and grades, it makes theoretical sense to add the chi-squares. When this is done, the total chi-square is significant at the .01 level. The table shows that differences in the three birth order categories are greater when there is no evidence of disinterest than when there is some evidence of disinterest. Since the original relationship between birth order and grades had been found to hold only for males (see Table 2), the parental interest control was applied separately for males and females. The results remain substantially the same: for males with no evidence of disinterest, the chi-square = 21.77, 4 df, $p < .001$; some evidence of disinterest $X^2 = 4.81$, 4 df, not significant. For females, no evidence of disinterest, $X^2 = 8.04$, 4df, $p < .10$; some evidence of disinterest, $X^2 = 4.56$, 4 df, not significant. The direction of the significant birth order effects was the same as in Table 1. From this comparison, it can be seen that when controlling for sex and parental interest, the relationship between birth order and grades is significant when there is no evidence of parental disinterest, but when there is evidence of disinterest, the relationship is not significant for either males or females.

We choose to interpret these results as offering partial support for hypothesis #3, but in a slightly different context than in which the hypothesis was stated. The results seem to suggest that it is not parental interest which makes the difference in academic performance, but parental disinterest. Rosenberg was impressed by the fact that very few respondents reported that their parents were not interested in them. Even with the liberal

Table 8 – Birth Order and Grades in Two Categories of Parental Interest

Grades	No Evidence of Disinterest			Some Evidence of Disinterest		
	Only	First-Born	Later-Born	Only	First-Born	Later-Born
High	60%	47	40	48	44	43
Medium	33	40	45	36	46	38
Low	7	13	15	16	14	19
Total Percent	100	100	100	100	100	100
Number	106	278	306	66	196	100

$X^2 = 15.26$, 4 df, p. $<.01$ $X^2 = 7.16$, 4 df, NS

Total $X^2 = 22.42$, 8 df, p. $<.01$

index of disinterest employed in this study, the effects of parental disinterest appear sufficient to substantially reduce the birth order effects on academic achievement. Parental interest, on the other hand, has no such effect. In this society, parental interest in one's children is normative. Because interest is normative and these normative expectations are met for most children, the variance in the birth order-academic performance relationship is probably not explicable within the parental interest context. Hence, we are led to conclude that at least for this sample, if the child's parents are perceived as being disinterested in him, the ordinal position he occupies matters little for academic performance. Yet given a normative parental interest, ordinal position is significant for academic performance.

In order to provide the clearest possible test of hypothesis #3, parental interest was considered from a slightly different perspective. The reader familiar with the work of Lasko (1954) may have been concerned with the operational definition of parental interest which has been formulated. Lasko has emphasized that it is not warm parental interest that is directed toward the first-born, but rather interference with and manipulation of the child. One possibility, then, is that the superior academic performance of first-borns is a result of parents' imposition of high standards on the child. Parents, being new at the game, impose unrealistic demands on the first-borns and then temper these demands with later-borns as their expectations become more reality oriented.[1]

Fortunately, the data at hand allow a comparison along these lines. One item on the questionnaire asked respondents whether their parents had placed more emphasis on high standards, on enjoying themselves, or had emphasized both equally. Table 9 indicates that the first-born respondents were slightly more likely to perceive parents as emphasizing enjoyment. In this case, only children report parental emphasis more similar to later-borns than to first-borns. The differences are not statistically significant. Overall, little support for Lasko's proposition is obtained.

However, since the results are in the direction predicted by Lasko, the findings can be applied to the relationship between birth order and grades. If the relationship is due to parental demands of high standards, controlling on this factor should equalize the tendency for first-borns and only children to report higher grades. It was not possible to make a comparison for each of the three alternative answers to the question concerning parental emphasis, since so few respondents reported that parents emphasized enjoying themselves. This is not a serious disadvantage, since our primary interest is in what happens when parents emphasize high standards. Table 10 indicates that when just those respondents whose parents emphasize high standards are compared, later-born children still report lower academic performance than either only children or first-born children. Thus, a definition of parental interest in terms of emphasis also fails to provide an elimination of the statistical tendency for first-born and only children to appear in the higher academic performance categories. Any conclusion must be stated tentatively, for the comparison is based upon an answer to only one question. Nevertheless, hypothesis #3 is not supported by redefining parental interest.

Table 9 — Birth Order and Parental Emphasis

Parents Emphasized	Only	First-Born	Later-Born
High Standards	27%	31	26
Enjoy Self	5	5	7
Both Equally	68	64	67
Total			
Percent	100	100	100
Number	190	565	712

$$X^2 = 6.21,\ 4\ df,\ NS$$

Table 10 - Birth Order and Grades of Respondents Who Report Parental Emphasis on High Standards

Grades	Only	First-Born	Later-Born
High	47%	48	36
Medium	38	41	42
Low	15	11	22
Total			
Percent	100	100	100
Number	47	164	172

$X^2 = 9.16$, 4 df, $p. < .10$

FOOTNOTES -- CHAPTER III

1. This suggestion was also made by Harris (1964: 39).

CHAPTER V

DISCUSSION AND CONCLUSIONS

The results of the study have implications both for the particular area of birth order research considered and for the topic as a whole. First, with respect to the specific hypotheses and their results, the following has been found:

Hypothesis #1: Self reports of academic performance will be highest for only children, next highest for first-born children, and lowest for later born children. The hypothesis was supported for males only, and differences between only and first-born males, while in the direction predicted, were not statistically significant.

Hypothesis #2: Evidence of parental disinterest will be highest for later-born children, and lowest for only children. (2a) The birth order differences will be greater for males than females. The second part of the hypothesis was not supported; males and females show little difference on the parental interest factor. Parental interest was found to be subject to the effects of family size, with birth order effects appearing only in the two child family. The proposition, we feel, should be modified to reflect this fact. Parental disinterest is significantly greater for the later-born child only in the two child family in the present sample.

Hypothesis #3: Holding parental interest constant, the relationship between birth order and academic performance will be eliminated or substantially reduced. The attenuation of birth order effects occurred in one category of parental interest and not in the other. This was interpreted as partial support for the hypothesis. The proposition, however, should be restated and given different meaning. When parental disinterest is held constant, the relationship between birth order and academic performance is substantially reduced. Holding parental interest constant, however, does not result in a reduction of the birth order effects on academic achievement. If anything, the birth order effects become more pronounced by removing those respondents who reported that their parents evidenced some disinterest in them.

The finding that birth order and academic performance are significantly related for males, but not for females, was not expected from the literature. In fact, the failure of other investigators to report such a sex difference leads to suspicion that it may lie in factors which have nothing to do with the interaction of ordinal position and sex of respondent. The comparisons show that later-born females are consistently lower in each grade category, but the differences are too small to reach statistical significance. One possible reason for this is that there is less total variability in the female distribution of grades than in the males. The sample reflects the often reported finding that girls consistently make better school records than boys. Consequently, fewer cases were in the lower grades category, and there was less opportunity for cases to depart from expectancy. This, plus the lack of any reason to predict sex differences, leads to the conclusion that the failure to obtain significant differences is not theoretically important. The direction of the findings are congruent with those of Elder (1962b), Sampson (1962), Schacter (1963) and Schoonover (1959).

The prediction that sex differences would exist for the relationship between parental disinterest and birth order was not supported. Yasuda (1964: 22) contends that siblings cannot be expected to be evenly distributed on educational attainment and social mobility irrespective of birth order, even in the United States. His data indicate that first-born males are more likely to obtain better jobs and higher education regardless of country of origin. This, we expected, would be translated into a difference of greater perceived parental disinterest on the part of female respondents. Our data do not necessarily conflict with the Yasuda study, despite the fact that no such tendency was evident. The present sample consisted of high school students in public schools, and there would have been little reason for parents to evidence the type of distinctions associated with sending some children to college and not others, or helping some to obtain training in the crafts and not others. If there is a translation of the factors mentioned by Yasuda into greater perceptions of disinterest on the part of females, it probably occurs later in life than the ages of our sample. However, Altus (1965: 874) found that first-born females as well as first-born males are overrepresented in college populations. We cannot, therefore, reject the posibility that the social-psychological effects of the first-born position are sufficient to overcome any male-female differentials for family resources in any age sample.

Using the symbolic interactionist perspective and findings on self-esteem, plus the speculations of a large number of investigators, we predicted a differential in parental disinterest greatest for later-borns and least for only children. The results supported the prediction, but we also found that birth order was unrelated to parental interest in larger families. The reason for controlling on family size was the possibility that parents in large families would be less likely to know all the child's friends or to be interested in what the child had to say merely because there were more children in the family. There is some doubt as to whether this is so, in retrospect, because reports of parental disinterest did not increase as family size increased (see Table 7).

One possible explanation may lie in the literature on large families. Bossard and Boll (1956) offer a comprehensive description of the ways in which large and small families differ. There are several indications that parent-child interaction differs qualitatively from that in the small family. Parenthood, they suggest, is of less emotional intensity in the large family. Discipline takes on a more impersonal, organizational character, with greater reliance on rules. The meaning which can be read into these characteristics is that position in the large family is less meaningful than in the small family. If rules are standardized, first-borns in large families may be less likely than first-borns in small families or only children to perceive differentials in parental interest. Whether these factors account for all, or even some of the reasons why the birth order effect is less evident in large families, the quality of parent-child interaction in varying family sizes will probably have to be taken into account. Again, our data cast doubt that the mere presence of more children accounts for the elimination of the birth order - parental interest relationship when controlling for family size.

Another possibility is that not only family size, but state of family development may be important. The first-born may begin with a considerable advantage in parental interest and attention, and gradually lose ground the longer the parents are married. The two-child family, on the average, would have been in existence a shorter period of time than the larger family, and could be one reason why the birth order effects showed up only for the former. Such a tendency for parents to gravitate toward more equal treatment of children in the family has not been demonstrated directly. One finding in the Lasko (1954) study implies such a possibility, however: "Parental behavior toward second children does not tend to change systematically as the child grows older. Systematic changes do occur in the treatment of first children, mainly in the direction of reduced parent-child interaction," (p. 136). Whether the tendency postulated above can be demonstrated empirically remains to be seen, but the control on family size provides results consistent with the implications of Lasko's study.

Interpretation of the third set of findings, birth order and academic performance controlled for parental interest, is rendered more difficult because of the nature of the data. Lacking an index of the degree of parental interest, the original relationship could be controlled in only two categories. Nevertheless, the controls produced strikingly different results in the two categories. Positional effects are not apparent for respondents who report some parental disinterest.

On the negative side, it was predicted that the effects of ordinal position would also disappear when comparing those respondents who did not report parental disinterest. As indicated earlier, this is probably the larger group in the population. Also, there was not apparent attenuation of birth order effects when controlling the parents' demands of high standards. These findings are the converse of our predictions and deserve comment.

Two dimensions of parental behavior have been considered in this study, which we can label for convenience parental interest and parental emphasis. Maccoby (1968: 248-251) has recently reviewed the accumulated knowledge on two analgous factors, which she considers as warmth-rejection and control-autonomy continuums. Summarizing the review, Maccoby contends "the main findings do indicate that the effects of one dimension cannot be understood except as the one dimension interacts with the other" (p. 251). Perhaps it is some combination of parental interest and parental demands for high standards that explains why only and first-born children are higher academic achievers.

There is also a question of variables intervening between parental interest and academic performance. Schacter (1959) has emphasized that first-borns are more likely to develop dependency patterns as a result of greater parental interest and monopoly of parents' time. This might logically produce an individual who is oriented favorably to adults and is interested in establishing a dependency type of relationship with them.

Several researchers have concluded that first-borns are indeed more adult oriented than later-borns. Palmer (1966) shows that first-borns have self-descriptions more similar to the self-descriptions of their parents than of their siblings. This finding goes hand in hand with the observation that first-borns are more responsive to normative influences (Amir et. al. 1968; Becker 1962, 1966; Simpson 1961; Wuebben 1967). If the grade-getter is one who can relate to authority figures (teachers), and use them as models for behavior, the data available would seem to indicate that the first-born fits this pattern quite well. The failure of our control on parental interest to produce the anticipated results of reducing the birth order - academic achievement relationship may be a reflection of the fact that parental interest is indirectly related to academic achievement, influencing factors such as self-concept and reference group orientations, which in turn are the more direct influences on academic performance. An interaction of positional effects with one or more intervening variables could conceivably change the nature of a birth order - dependent variable relationship.

Several points in the above discussion could be taken as suggestions for the extension of the present research. If this study has been able to suggest that parental interest is a meaningful conception for the study of birth order, at least three questions arise for which there are at present no answers.

First, it was suggested in Chapter II that position in the family may mean something very different with various sex combinations of siblings. Although parent-child interaction has been the major focus in the present study, any attempt at refinement of the suggested relationships would be well advised to consider sex of siblings. As a beginning, one design within feasibility with survey techniques might consider whether the advantage of the first-born male with respect to parental interest varies when the younger sib is male or female.

Secondly, the study suggests that parental interest is too general to be of utility as an explanation. A correlation study of the effects of both degree of parental interest, and degree to which parents emphasize high standards would be useful. Ideally, some measure of the interaction of these factors would provide the most useful knowledge.

Finally, there is an indication that effects of ordinal position may be altered by variables intervening between the processes underlying the position in the family and the dependent variables of interest. For example, we assumed a time sequence in the present study of: Birth Order → Parental Interest → Academic Performance. Depending on the nature of the data, such assumptions may have to be made before the interrelationships of the variables can be explored at all. However, the results of the present study, combined with the research of Rosenberg (1965), and the assumptions of symbolic interactionism suggest that a more realistic pattern may be: Birth Order → Parental Interest → Self-Esteem → Academic Performance. Furthermore, there is no reason to believe that the causal chain runs in only one direction. Academic performance should have an effect on self-esteem, and both variables probably influence parental interest. The next logical extension of the present study along these lines would seem to be a multi-variate design that could accommodate intervening variables (and here there is no reason to suspect that self-esteem is the only important variable - peer relations, or reference group orientations in general are undoubtedly significant[1]) and specify how they vary together.

The question of intervening variables is one point which has considerable significance for the area of birth order research as a whole. Based on the low size of correlations of ordinal position with almost any dependent variable, we are led to conclude that birth order accounts for a very small percentage of the variance. However, when we consider that position in the family may influence the way parents may react to a child, which may in turn influence other variables, and so on, the total effect of position in the family may far exceed that which we attribute on the basis of a direct comparison. At present, there is insufficient data to estimate what might be the total effects of position upon socialization and personality.[2]

FOOTNOTES -- CHAPTER IV

1. Rose (1956) has shown that family size is related to reference group rankings. It seems likely that ordinal position is also an influence in the choice of a reference group hierarchy.

2. This observation was made by Dr. Edward Z. Dager, National Science Foundation, in a conversation with the writer.

APPENDIX A

BIRTH ORDER RESEARCH BY SUBJECT AREA AND FINDINGS

Area	Studies	Conclusion(s)
Achievement	Elder (1962a); Koch (1954); Nisbet (1961); Jones (1954); Pierce (1959); Rosen (1961); Sampson (1962); Schacter (1963); Schoonover (1959); Visher (1948); West (1960).	First-borns show greater academic motivation and achievement. First-borns are more likely to become scientists.
Affiliation	Conners (1963); Dember (1963); Radloff (1961); Sarnoff (1961); Schacter (1959); Schooler & Scarr (1962); Zimbardo (1963); Weiss (1966); Helmreich & Collins (1967); Wrightsman (1960).	Desire to affiliate under conditions of anxiety threat or fear is greater for first-borns.
Alcoholism	Bakan (1949); de Luit (1964); Navratil (1959); Smart (1963).	First-borns are slightly underrepresented in populations of alcoholics.
Anxiety	Gerard & Rabbie (1961); Staples & Walters (1961); Vernon et. al. (1967); Weller (1962); Wrightsman (1960); Yaryan (1961).	No conclusion. Three studies show first-borns more anxious, two show no birth order effects, one shows first-born females more anxious, first-born males less anxious.
Behavior Problems	Cushna et. al. (1964); Damrin (1949); Eisenman & Taylor (1966); Haeberle (1959); McFarlane et. al. (1954).	First-borns are more likely to have dependency problems. Later-borns are overrepresented in schizophrenic patterns. Findings are inconsistent on withdrawal and inter-analyzing patterns.
College Attendance	Bayer (1966); Schacter (1963); Smelser (1968).	First-borns are more likely to attend college.

Area	Studies	Conclusion(s)
Conformity	Amir et. al. (1968); Becker (1962, 1966), Simpson (1961); Palmer (1966).	First-born are more responsive to normative influences.
Creativity	Datta (1968); Eisenmann (1964); Harris (1964).	No conclusion. One study shows later-borns are more creative, one shows first-borns are more creative, one shows no difference.
Frustrations (Reactions to)	Glass et. al. (1963).	Later-borns react with greater annoyance to a frustrating agent.
Honesty	Wuebben (1967).	First-borns are more honest.
Intelligence	Schoonover (1959); Jones (1956); Koch (1959)*; Thurstone & Jenkins (1932).	First-borns initially score higher on verbal intelligence tests. No birth order difference in intelligence in post-school years.
Juvenile Delinquency	Sletto (1934).	First-borns are overrepresented in delinquency rates.
Marriage	Heiss (1960); Kemper (1966).	First-borns are most likely to marry within the same religious faith. There is no evidence of birth order homogamy.
Occupational Choice	Baker (1963); Koch (1956b).	First-borns are overrepresented in parent-surrogate occupations (e.g. teaching, nursing).
Personality Traits	Kammeyer (1966); McArthur (1956); Palmer (1956); Ray-Chowdbury (1965); Rosenberg (1965).	First-borns are more likely to be: conservative, adult-oriented, responsible, serious, manipulative, introverted. Later-borns are more likely to be: optimistic, extroverted, peer-oriented, independent, aggressive. Only children have the highest self-esteem.

Area	Studies	Conclusion(s)
Popularity with:		
a. Peers	Alexander (1966); Dittes (1961); Koch (1956a); Schacter (1964).	No conclusion. Two studies find first-borns less popular, but a more controlled study finds first-borns more popular.
b. Adults	Koch (1955).	First-borns are rated higher by adults.
Role & Sex-Role Identification	Rosenberg & Sutton-Smith (1954); Stotland & Dunn (1962).	Later-borns empathize and identify to a greater extent than do first-borns and onlies.
Social Mobility	Alexander (1968); Svalastoga (1959); Yasuda (1964).	There is a slight tendency for first-borns to be upwardly mobile to a greater extent than later-borns.
Suicide	Lester (1966).	No conclusion.
Volunteering	Capra & Dittes (1962); Suedfeld (1964); Dember (1964); Ward (1964).*	First-borns are overrepresented among volunteers for experiments.

* Studies show results which conflict with conclusions drawn.

APPENDIX B - PARENTAL INTEREST INDEX

<u>Questionnaire Instructions:</u> WE WOULD NOW LIKE YOU TO THINK BACK TO A SPECIFIC PERIOD OF YOUR CHILDHOOD, NAMELY WHEN YOU WERE IN THE 5TH AND 6TH GRADES. FOR MOST CHILDREN THIS WOULD BE ABOUT THE AGE OF 10 AND 11. TRY TO KEEP THIS PERIOD GENERALLY IN MIND WHEN ANSWERING THE FOLLOWING QUESTIONS. ALTHOUGH YOUR FEELINGS AND EXPERIENCES MAY HAVE VARIED, TRY TO ANSWER THE QUESTIONS IN TERMS OF YOUR AVERAGE OR TYPICAL EXPERIENCES AT THIS TIME.

Parental Interest

Item 1. During this period did your mother know who most of your friends were?
- 1 ____ Knew who all of them were
- 2 ____ Knew who most of them were
- *3 ____ Knew who some of them were
- *4 ____ Knew none, or almost none, of them

Item 2. During this period did your father know who most of your friends were?
- 1 ____ Knew who all of them were
- 2 ____ Knew who most of them were
- *3 ____ Knew who some of them were
- *4 ____ Knew none, or almost none of them

Item 3. As far as you can tell, how interested are the other family members in what you have to say in mealtime conversations?
- 1 ____ Very interested
- 2 ____ Fairly interested
- *4 ____ Not interested

*A "positive" response to any one or more of these items was scored as some evidence of parental disinterest.

Parental Emphasis

Which would you say was more important to your parents – that you meet high standards of performance or that you enjoy yourself while you're young?

- 1 ____ Meet high standards
- 2 ____ Enjoy self
- 3 ____ Both equally important

BIBLIOGRAPHY

Ordinal Position and Socialization

Books

Bossard, J.H.S. and E.S. Boll, <u>The Large Family System</u>. Philadelphia: U. of Pennsylvania Press, 1956

Coopersmith, S., <u>The Antecedents of Self-Esteem</u>. San Francisco: W.H. Freeman & Co., 1967

Douglas, J.W.B., <u>The Home and the School: A Study of Ability and Attainment in the Primary School</u>. London: MacGibbon and Kee, 1964.

Harris, I., <u>The Promised Seed</u>. Glencoe, Ill: The Free Press, 1964.

Rosenberg, M., <u>Society and the Adolescent Self-Image</u>. Princeton: Princeton Univ. Press, 1965

Schacter, S., <u>The Psychology of Affiliation</u>. Stanford: Stanford Univ. Press, 1959

Sears, R.R., E.E. Macoby and H. Levin, Patterns of Child Rearing. Evanston, Ill: Row, Peterson & Co., 1957

Sutton-Smith, B., and B.G. Rosenberg, <u>The Sibling</u>. New York: Holt, Rinehart & Winston, 1970

Svalastoga, Kaare, <u>Prestige, Class and Mobility</u>. London: William Reinemann, 1959

Thurstone, L.L. and R.L. Jenkins, <u>Order of Birth, Parent Age, and Intelligence</u>. Chicago: Univ. of Chicago Press, 1932

Turner, R., <u>The Social Context of Ambition</u>. San Francisco: Chandler Publication Co., 1964

Vuyk, R., Das Kind in der Zweikenderfamilie. Stuggart, Germany: Hans Ruber, 1959

Articles

Adams, B.N., "Birth Order and College Attendance: A Re-Evaluation of a Re-Evaluation," *Sociometry*, 1969, 32, 503-504

Alexander, N.C., "Ordinal Position and Sociometric Status," *Sociometry*, 1966, 29, 41-51

_____, "Ordinal Position and Social Mobility," *Sociometry*, 1968, 31, 285-293

Altus, W.D., "Birth Order and Its Sequalae," *Intl. J. of Psychiatry*, 1967, 3, 23-32

_____, "Birth Order and Academic Primogeniture," *J. Pers. Soc. Psych.*, 1965, 2, 872-876

Amir, Y., S. Sharan, and Y. Kovarsky, "Birth Order, Family Structure and Avoidance Behavior," *J. Pers. Soc. Psych.*, 1968, 10, 271-278

Arrowwood, A.J. and D.N. Amoroso, "Social Comparison and Ordinal Position," *J. Pers. Soc. Psych.*, 1965, 2, 101-104

Bakan, D., "The Relationship between Alcoholism and Birth Rank," *Quart. J. of Studies on Alcohol*, 1949, 10, 434-440

Baker, S.R., "Relationship of Selection of Nursing as a Vocation to Birth Order," *Nursing Research*, 1963, 12, 248-249

Bayer, S.E., "Birth Order and College Attendance," *J. Marr. and Family*, 1966, 28, 480-484

_____, "Birth Order and Attainment of the Doctorate: A Test of Economic Hypotheses," *Amer. J. Soc.*, 1967, 72, 540-550

_____, and J.K. Folger, "The Current State of Birth Order Research," *Intl. J. of Psychiatry*, 1967, 3, 37-39

Becker, S.W. and J. Carroll, "Ordinal Position and Conformity," *J. Abnorm. Soc. Psych.*, 1962, 65, 129-131

_____, M.J. Lerner and J. Carroll, "Conformity as a Function of Birth Order and Type of Group Pressure," *J. Pers. Soc. Psych.*, 1966, 3, 242-244

_____, M.J. Lerner and J. Carroll, "Conformity as a Function of Birth Order Payoff and Type of Group Pressure," *J. Abnorm. Soc. Psych.*, 1964, 69, 318-323

Bossard, J.H.S., "Family Modes of Expression," *Amer. Soc. Rev.*, 1945, 10, 226-237

Bradley, R.E. and M.P. Sanborn, "Ordinal Position of High School Students Identified by Their Teachers as Superior," *J. of Ed. Psych.*, 1969, 60, 41-45

Bragg, B.W. and V.L. Allen, "Ordinal Position and Conformity: A Role Theory Analysis," *Sociometry*, 1970, 33, 371-381

Brim, O.G. Jr., "Family Structure and Sex-Role Learning by Children," *Sociometry*, 1958, 21, 1-16

Capra, P.C. and J.E. Dittes, "Birth Order as a Selective Factor Among Volunteer Subjects," *J. Abnorm. Soc. Psych.*, 1962, 64, 302

Carrigan, W.C. and J.W. Julian, "Sex and Birth Order Differences in Conformity as a Function of Need Affiliation Arousal," *J. Pers. Soc. Psych.*, 1966, 3, 479-482

Clausen, J.A., "Family Structure and Personality," in L.W. Hoffman and M.L. Hoffman (eds), *Review of Child Development Research*, Vol. II. New York: Russell Sage Foundation, 1966, 1-53

_____, "Family Size and Birth Order as Influences upon Socialization and Personality: Bibliography and Abstracts," (mimeo), Social Science Research Council, 1965

_____, "Perspectives on Childhood Socialization," in *Socialization and Society*. Boston: Little, Brown & Co., 1968, 130-181

Conners, C.K., "Birth Order and Needs for Affiliation," *J. of Personality*, 1963, 31, 408-416

Cushna, B.M., M. Green and B.C.F. Snider, "First Born and Last Born Children in a Child Development Clinic," *J. Indiv. Psych.*, 1964, 20, 179-182

Dager, E.Z., "Socialization and Personality Development in the Child," in H.T. Christensen (ed.), *Handbook of Marriage and the Family*, Chicago: Rand-McNally, 1964, 740-781

Damrin, D.E., "Family Size and Sibling Age, Sex and Position as Related to Certain Aspects of Adjustment," *J. of Social Psych.*, 1949, 29, 93-102

Datta, L., "Birth Order and Potential Scientific Creativity," *Sociometry*, 1968, 31, 76-88

Davis, A., "American Status Systems and the Socialization of the Child," *Amer. Soc. Rev.*, 1941, 6, 345-354

de Luit, J.E.E., "Alcoholism, Birth Order and Socializing Agents," *J. Abnorm. Soc. Psych.*, 1964, 69, 457-458

Dember, W.N., "Birth Order and Need Affiliation," *Amer. Psychologist*, 1968 18, 356

Dittes, J.E., "Birth Order and Vulnerability to Differences in Acceptance," *Amer. Psychologist*, 1961, 16, 358

Eisenman, R., "Birth Order and Artistic Creativity," *J. Indiv. Psych.*, 1964, 20, 183-185

Eisenman, R., "Birth Order, Self-Esteem, and Prejudice Against the Physically Disabled," *J. Indiv. Psych.*, 1970, 26, 147-156

_____, and R.E. Taylor, "Birth Order and MMPI Patterns," *J. Indiv. Psych.*, 1966, 22, 208-211

Elder, G.H. Jr., "Family Structure: The Effects of Size of Family, Sex Composition and Ordinal Position on Academic Motivation and Achievement," in *Adolescent Achievement and Mobility Aspirations* (mineo). Chapel Hill, NC: Institute for Research in Social Science, 1962a, 59-72

_____, "Structural Variations in the Child Rearing Relationship," *Sociometry*, 1962b, 25, 241-262

Exner, J.E. Jr., and B. Sutton-Smith, "Birth Order and Hierarchal Versus Innovative Role Requirements," *J. of Personality*, 1970, 28, 581-587

Gerard, H.B. and J.M. Rabbie, "Fear and Social Comparison," *J. Abnorm. Soc. Psych.*, 1961, 62, 586-592

Glass, D.C., M. Horowitz and I. Firestone, "Birth Order and Reactions to Frustration," *J. Abnorm. Soc. Psych.*, 1963, 66, 192-195

Green, E.J., "Birth Order, Parental Interest and Academic Performance," Paper read at Southern Sociological Society Meeting, Atlanta, 1970

Haeberle, A.W., "Interactions of Sex, Birth Order and Dependency with Behavior Problems and Symptons in Emotionally Disturbed Pre-School Children," Paper read at Eastern Psychological Assn. Meeting, Philadelphia, 1958

Heiss, J.S., "Premarital Characteristics of the Religiously Inter-married in an Urban Area," *Amer. Soc. Rev.*, 1960, 25, 47-55

Hare, R.T. and P.A. Hare, "Social Correlates of Autonomy for Nigerian University Students," J. of Soc. Psych., 1968, 76, 163-168

Harris, I.E. and K.I. Howard, "Birth Order and Responsibility," J. of Marr. & Fam., 1968, 30, 427-432

Helmreich, R.L. and B.E. Collins, "Situational Determinants of Affiliation Preference Under Stress," J. Pers. Soc. Psych., 1967, 6, 79-85

_____, D. Kuiken and B. Collins, "Effects of Stress and Birth Order on Attitude Change," J. of Personality, 1968, 36, 466-473

Heilbrun, A. Jr., and D. Fromme, "Parental Identification of Late Adolescents and Level of Adjustment: The Importance of Parent-Model Attributes, Ordinal Position, and Sex of Child," J. Genetic Psych., 1965, 107, 49-59

Henry, A.F., "Sibling Structure and Perception of the Disciplinary Roles of Parents," Sociometry, 1957, 20, 67-74

Jones, E.S., "College Graduates and Their Later Success," U. of Buffalo Studies, 1956, 22, 185

Jones, H.E., "Order of Birth," in C. Murchinson (ed.), A Handbook of Child Psychology. Worchester, Mass: Clark U. Press, 1933, 551-589

_____, "The Environment and Mental Development," in L. Carmichael (ed.), Manual of Child Psychology. New York: Wiley, 1954

Kammeyer, K., "Birth Order and the Feminine Sex Role Among College Women," Amer. Soc. Rev., 1966, 31, 508-515

_____, "Birth Order as a Research Variable," Soc. Forces, 1967, 46, 71-80

Kemper, T.D., "Mate Selection and Marital Satisfaction According to Sibling Type of Husband and Wife," J. Marr. & Fam., 1966, 28, 346-349

Koch, H.L., "The Relation of Primary Mental Abilities in Five and Six Year Olds to Sex of Child and Characteristics of His Sibling," Child Development, 1955, 26, 13-40

_____, "The Relation of Certain Family Constellation Characteristics and the Attitudes of Children Toward Adults," Child Development, 1954, 25, 209-223

_____, "Attitudes of Young Children Toward Their Peers as Related to Certain Characteristics of Their Siblings," Psych. Monographs, 1956a, 70, 1-41

_____, "Children's Work Attitudes and Sibling Characteristics," Child Development, 1956b, 27, 289-310

Krinsky, S.G., "The Relationship Among Birth Order, Dimensions of Independence-Dependence and Choice of a Scientific Career," in W.W. Cooley (ed.), Career Development of Scientists: An Overlapping Longitudinal Study. Cambridge: Harvard Univ. Grad School of Ed., 1963, 157-170

Lasko, J.K., "Parent Behavior toward First and Second Children," Genetic Psych. Monographs, 1954, 49, 96-137

Lester, D., "Sibling Position and Suicidal Behavior," J. Indiv. Psych., 1966, 22, 204-207

Macfarland, J.W., L. Allen and M.P. Hanzik, "A Developmental Study of the Behavior Problems of Normal Children Between 21 Months and 14 Years," U. of Calif. Publication in Child Development, Vol. II, Berkeley, Calif: U. of Calif. Press, 1954

McArthur, C., "Personalities of First and Second Children," Psychiatry, 1956, 19, 47-54

McDonald, A.P. Jr., "Manifestations of Different Levels of Socialization by Birth Order," Dev. Psych., 1969, 1, 485-492

Mehta, P.H. and S. Juneja, "Birth Order, Vocational Preference and Vocational Expectation," Indian J. of Psych., 1969, 46, 57-70

Navratil, L., "On the Etiology of Alcohol," Quart. J. of Studies on Alcohol, 1959, 20, 236-244

Nisbet, J., "Family Environment and Intelligence," in A.H. Halsey (ed.), Education, Economy and Society. New York: The Free Press, 1961, 273-287

Palmer, R.D., "Birth Order and Identification," J. Consult. Psych., 1966, 30, 129-135

Phillips, E.L., "Cultural vs. Intrapsychic Factors in Childhood behavior Problem Referrals," J. of Clinical Psych., 1956, 12, 400-401

Pierce, J.V., "The Educational Motivation Patterns of Superior Students Who Do and Do Not Achieve in High School," Report of U.S. Office of Education. Department of Health, Education and Welfare. Univ. of Chicago, November, 1959

Platt, J.J., R. Eisenmann and E. Degross, "Birth Order and Sex Differences in Future Time Perspective," Dev. Psych., 1969, 1, 70

Price, J., "Personality Differences Within Families: Comparison of Adult Brothers and Sisters," J. of Biosocial Science, 1969, 1, 177-205

Raboch, J. and V. Bartak, " Das Sexualleben frigider Frauen," (The Sexual Life of Frigid Women) Psychiatrie, Neurologie und Medizinische Psychologie, 1968, 20, 368-373

Radloff, R., "Opinion Evaluation and Affiliation," J. Abnorm. Soc. Psych., 1961, 62, 578-585

Ray-Chowdbury, K., "Birth Order and the Motives of Life," Indian Soc. Bulletin, 1965, 2, 150-160

Rose, Arnold M., "Reference Groups of Rural High School Youth," Child Development, 1956, 27, 351-363

Rosen, B.C., "Family Structure and Achievement Motivation," Amer. Soc. Rev., 1961, 26, 574-585

Roseberg, B.G., and B. Sutton-Smith, "Ordinal Position and Sex Role Identification, Genetic Psych. Monographs, 1964, 70, 297-328

Sampson, E.E., "Birth Order, Need Achievement and Conformity," J. Abnorm. Soc. Psych., 1962, 64, 155-159

_____, "The Study of Ordinal Position: Antecedents and Outcomes," in B. Maher (ed.), Progress in Experimental Personality Research, Vol. II. New York: Academic Press, 1965, 175-228

_____, and F.T. Hancock, "An Examination of the Relationship Between Ordinal Position, Personality and Conformity: An Extension, Replication and Partial Verification," J. Pers. Soc. Psych., 1967, 5, 398-407

Sarnoff, I. and P.G. Zimbardo, "Anxiety, Fear and Social Affiliation," J. Abnorm. Soc. Psych., 1961, 62, 356-363

Schacter, S.S., "Birth Order, Eminence and Higher Education," Amer. Soc. Rev., 1963, 28, 757-767

_____, "Birth Order and Sociometric Choice," J. Abnorm. Soc. Psych., 1964, 68, 453-456

Schooler, C., "Birth Order and Schizophrenia," A.M.A. Archives of General Psychiatry, 1961, 4, 91-97

_____, and S. Scarr, "Affiliation among Chronic Schizophrenics: Relation to Intrapersonal and Birth Order Factors," J. of Personality, 1962, 30, 178-192

Schoonover, S.M., "The Relationship of Intelligence and Achievement to Birth Order, Sex of Sibling, and Age Interval," J. of Ed. Psych., 1959, 50, 143-146

Sears, P.S., "Doll Play Aggression in Normal Young Children: Influence of Sex, Age, Sibling Status, Father's Absence," Psych. Monographs, 1851, 65, whole #323

Sears, R.R., "Ordinal Position in the Family as a Psychological Variable," Amer. Soc. Rev., 1950, 15, 397-401

Sechrest, L. and L. Flores, "Sibling Position of Philippine Psychiatric Patients," J. of Soc. Psych., 1969, 77, 135-137

Shrader, W.K. and T. Leventhal, "Birth Order of Children and Parental Report of Problems," Child Development, 1968, 39, 1164-1175

Singer, J.E., "The Use of Manipulative Strategies: Machiavellianism and Attractiveness," Sociometry, 1964, 27, 128-150

Sletto, R.F., "Sibling Position and Juvenile Delinquency," Amer. J. Soc., 1934, 39, 657-669

Smart, R.G., "Alcoholism, Birth Order and Family Size," J. Abnorm. Soc. Psych., 1963, 66, 17-23

_____, "Social Group Membership, Leadership, and Birth Order," J. Soc. Psych., 1965, 67, 221-225

Smelser, W.T., "Where Are the Siblings? A Reevaluation of the Relationship Between Birth Order and College Attendance," Sociometry, 1968, 31, 294-303

Staples, F.R. and R.H. Walters, "Anxiety, Birth Order, and Susceptibility to Social Influence," J. Abnorm. Soc. Psych., 1961, 62, 716-179

Stotland, E. and R.E. Dunn, "Identification, 'Oppositeness', Authoritarianism, Self-Esteem and Birth Order," J. Abnorm. Soc. Psych., 1963, 66, 532-540

_____, and R.E. Dunn, "Empathy, Self-Esteem and Birth Order," Psych. Monographs, 1963, 76, 1-21

Stotland, E. and J.A. Walsh, "Birth Order and an Experimental Study of Empathy," J. Abnorm. Soc. Psych., 1963, 66, 610-614

Stroup, A. and K.J. Hunter, "Sibling Position in the Family and Personality of Offspring," J. Marr. & Fam., 1965, 27, 65-68

Stout, A.M., "Parent Behavior toward Children of Different Ordinal Positions and Sibling Status," Unpublished Ph. D. dissertation, U. of Calif., Berkeley, 1960

Suedfeld, P., "Birth Order and Volunteers for Sensory Deprivation," J. Abnorm. Soc. Psych., 1964, 68, 195-196

Sutton-Smith, B., J.M. Roberts and B.G. Rosenberg, "Sibling Associations and Role Involvement," Merrill-Palmer Quarterly, 1964, 10, 25-38

_____, B.G. Rosenberg and F. Landy, "Father-Absence Effects in Families of Different Sibling Compositions," Child Development, 1968, 39, 1213-1221

Tomeh, A.K., "Birth Order and Kinship Affiliation," J. Marr. & Fam., 1969, 31, 19-26

_____, "Birth Order and Friendship Association," J. Marr. & Fam., 1970, 32, 360-369

Varela, J.A., "A Cross-Cultural Replication of an Experiment Involving Birth Order," J. Abnorm. Soc. Psych., 1964, 69, 456-457

Verger, D., "Birth Order and Sibling Differences in Interests," J. Indiv. Psych., 1968, 24, 56-62

Vernon, D.T.A., J.M. Foley and J.L. Schulman, "Effect of Mother-Child Separation and Birth Order on Young Children's Responses to Two Potentially Stressful Experiences," J. Pers. Soc. Psych., 1967, 5, 162-174

Visher, S.S., "Environmental Backgrounds of Leading American Scientists," Amer. Soc. Rev., 1948, 13, 65-72

Ward, C.D., "A Further Examination of Birth Order as a Selective Factor Among Volunteer Subjects," J. Abnorm. Soc. Psych., 1964, 69, 311-313

Warren, J.R., "Birth Order and Social Behavior," Psych. Bull., 1966, 65, 38-49

Weiss, R.L., "Some Determinants of Emitted Reinforcing Behavior: Listener Reinforcement and Birth Order," J. Pers. Soc. Psych., 1966, 3, 489-492

Weller, L., "The Relationship of Birth Order to Anxiety: A Replication of the Schacter Findings," Sociometry, 1962, 25, 415-417

West, S.S., "Sibling Configurations of Scientists," Amer. J. Soc., 1960, 66, 268-274

Wrightsman, L.S. Jr., "Effects of Waiting with Others on Changes in Level of Felt Anxiety," J. Abnorm. Soc. Psych., 1960, 61, 216-222

Wuebben, P.L., "Honesty of Subjects and Birth Order," J. Pers. Soc. Psych., 1967, 5, 350-352

Yaryan, R.B. and L. Festinger, "Preparatory Action and Belief in the Probable Occurence of Future Events," J. Abnorm. Soc. Psych., 1961, 63, 603-606

Yasuda, S., "A Methodological Inquiry into Social Mobility," Amer. Soc. Rev., 1964, 29, 16-23

Zimbardo, P. and R. Formica, "Emotional Comparison and Self-Esteem," J. of Personality, 1963, 31, 141-162